No Easy Light

Also by Susan Sibbet

Under Suspicion of Sisters

Burnt Toast and Other Recipes

Suspensions

Also from Sixteen Rivers Press

difficult news, by Valerie Berry

Translations from the Human Language, by Terry Ehret

Snake at the Wrist, by Margaret Kaufman

Sacred Precinct, by Jacqueline Kudler

What I Stole, by Diane Sher Lutovich

After Cocteau, by Carolyn Miller

Falling World, by Lynn Lyman Trombetta

SUSAN SIBBET

No Easy Light

Sixteen Rivers Press
SAN FRANCISCO

Printed in the United States of America

I would like to thank the following publications, in which some of the poems in this book first appeared: *A Small Box of Poets* (Protean Press), *Berkeley Poets Co-op, Bernal Journal,* California Poets in the Schools anthologies (1988, 1995, 2000), *Chocolate* (Chronicle Books), *Cycles of the Moon, Doula, If Poetry, The Napa Review, paragraph, Poetry San Francisco, The Stereopticon, VIVO,* and *Woman Poet West.*

I owe many thanks to Soapstone, to the Headlands Center for the Arts, and to the Bunting Institute for the residencies and fellowships that helped me to write the poems in this book. Special thanks to Jane Anne Staw, and to all the members of the press for their many helpful conversations and suggestions.

Most of all, my deepest love to Carolyn Miller and Terry Ehret, for their generous wisdom and friendship.

Special thanks to Mervyn's/Target Stores for their support of Sixteen Rivers.

Design: Patricia Koren of Kajun Design, San Francisco, California
Cover photograph: "Front Stairs, Afternoon Light," by David Sibbet

Library of Congress Control Number: 2003098599
ISBN 0-9707370-6-8

For David

and for Thom, Valentine, Jerda, and Phil

and for all my sisters, everywhere

Contents

Still This Voice

Voice

my voice
darker
struggling with light
too light   two lights
nights
these nights
        sleeping without
            voice

tonight
we make our own light
    two lights
    two voices

this light night
giving voice
voice giving shadow

the voice a shadow
to what the brain
    desires
being everywhere
all over the body

voice   light
    shadow   voice
still this voice

Here,

what we know, perhaps what matters,
is mock orange and bright acacia in spring,
small folded bloom, the secret flowers
of sweet gum in summer,
the slow winter rains.

In this still, warm air,
the heavy days like spoons of jam,
my tongue will never get used to the tickling.
Today, I knew an earthquake would come to shake me
before it began. On the phone
with my friend across the city,
talking of our children, she asked me if I felt it,
before it began to shake this house.

Here, they built on sand, using what was left
of the old redwoods for the crossbeams.
The smaller trees that my great-grandfather
in Ukiah passed by, we use to build decks
on the backs of houses, to get the view
of the yard behind.

Here there is no groundwater, no easy light,
our own roots are the enemy, stealing from
each other. Counting the spoons,
we are waiting, each of us, and getting older.
We count everything now.

Pearl Harbor, Territory of Hawaii, 1951

On the Base,
everywhere was where she
wasn't supposed to be.

The roads were empty: black tarmac, no sidewalks,
rusted wire fences. In the close quarters, we
listened to them next door, wailing, spanking, silent.

It was easier to get in if a building was left
open, the side door of the Base chapel; unnoticed, she
could slip into the hot, dusty rooms—

silent light between the blinds, the confession closets,
white robes, velvet basins, golden cups—stealing
crayons from Sunday school cabinets left unlocked.

She pushed open the heavy doors of Fleet Headquarters,
followed where the fathers went, her heart pounding though
no one noticed her in those busy rooms, soft sounds of fans,

khaki men talking on the telephone in low voices,
pale women walking past carrying papers, heels
clicking down the dark gray linoleum halls.

She went under the barbed wire fence, across
the artillery range, down the cliff to the shallow cave
some boys had found behind stinging vines.

In the dark, a cobweb smell, dead leaves, a worn-out
broom, some sort of dented, blackened cook pan the boys said
a Jap soldier had left behind when he hid there, never

knowing that the war was over. Maybe he was still there, or maybe the boys had found a bit of bone, a finger joint—she ran away before they could make her cry.

Moving Day

In this sediment and grainy condensation,
the emptied room holds more than swept dust.
Toast crumbs, one broken pencil remain behind,
as in the habit of long division.

The emptied room holds more than swept dust.
Silence remainders the layers of interest, the smallest piece,
as in the habit of long division.
Button, marble, red checker—the lost parts collect.

Silence remainders the layers of interest, the smallest piece,
what I will recall after the change of address.
Button, marble, red checker—the lost parts collect,
placed in any unmarked box along with the rest.

What I will recall after the change of address:
the revelation of motes dazzles.
Placed in any unmarked box along with the rest,
a hollow light remains with its bright echo.

The revelation of motes dazzles.
Wait for the silence alone. Remember:
A hollow light will remain with its bright echo
in this sediment, this grainy condensation.

In Silence a Couple

In their silence a couple drives to the airport
watching the light change over San Bruno Mountain.

The man stops his dream at this point of accomplishment;
the woman is filled only with her fears. The pressure

of the green world holds firm against the sky, and
stars, clouds, mist, rain, even the pink gel of dawn hurts.

In the soft haze each new thing in its new light passes by.
The Mission Blues unfold from their cocoons

among the blue lupine found only here,
and here they are lost in the bulldozer scrapings.

A cat may be driven by desire into the highway,
nature turning on itself from within.

Quills, spines, point by point, a porcupine has thin barbs
held inside the body at the anchor point,

quills it may just shake off,
and the motion of disturbance is release.

Even cut off by neap tide, the spiny sea urchin will extrude,
reach through its shield, return on individual points as

slowly as a thorn hedge would move, back into shivered
tide pools glittering in the rocks below the highway.

And if a sea cucumber could watch, if it had eyes to see, hanging
there without risk, no edges, inside and

out, a live, unsensing Möbius strip,
then what would hurt? Not

that body, unregenerative surface
sucking rock.

Slow, Listening

So many dead creatures here
close by the highway,
we see their flat bodies
stiff and dry.

Are they all gone
in this hurrying world?

We take the highway
to slow down, walk
along the river
down from the falls.

Are they all
in this hurrying

For early summer, the river's low,
rushing past the rocks,
a hush along the trail. I hear
in the leaves

Are they
in this

an awkward rustle
and then quiet,
something there,
holding still.

Are they

I stop,
wait, until
my eyes can see
in the shadow

they

a darker lump, big, bigger
than I thought; not
a bird hiding, it was
rough, black, glistening,

the

it was listening sideways
waiting so still,
an eye, a webbed foot
bunched under the dark

of the rock, waiting

Sowbug Virtue

It comes, the feared.
Held, I bend,

curl, overlap
myself, center, and

dropped,
shot away in a

ping, rolling
along the sidewalk,

under the leaf, between
bricks,

away from sight. I,
invisible,

I believe, yet so often
wrong. I hurt

no one. Only,
my un-

importance should save
me. I don't

eat all   like snails,
monsters of the spiral

stomachs. I don't
bite, or prick or

poison, I eat
leftovers, clean up mess.

I uncurl, survive,
wave feelers, feet,

what's a leg or two?
Still enough to

hump along
all day until

the shadow, then
I watch the moths,

joyful
and safe

in their cold
high dark

Waking, the alarm, and

I lie still in clean and empty sheets,
my body divided into four parts.
I am trying to bring them toward one another
in their proper order.
Above the handsome thorax of the queen,
the sturdy elephant legs,
the prehensile tail of the New World,
the lioness raises her smooth and brutal head.

How do my cells touch each other, connect
as flesh? How do they spread,
shoulder, torso, pelvis?
Are my feet dreaming as they curl and uncurl?
My fingers smooth the flat of the mattress.

I can shift the parts toward each other
and they send up the results—
warmth, slow fullness, the smooth
inside of a shell, some other
material, hidden skin or blood under the surface—
not what I expect,
the roaring inside the ear, the flattened
hairs rising under the sound. Now
lips, fingers, the hollow of the slightly
bent elbow, the tendons of the heel
hardly know each other
except by sensation.
Uneven welts join the four, scar
tissue netted lines marking off the parts.
I will not dress in the light.

The Very Thing

A mistranslation from Eugenio Montale's "La Verita"

The very thing isn't a thing like a rosy rose.
It's some tarlike essence, topic of the gods.
Not some pulverized bits of tiny cassettes disguised
by ambient sound persons
and not some piece of the cross of god "granulated"
by well-known stage persons.
The very thing is a zone of sediment, of tiny wristlike bones,
not a sharp word-sickness in god's dialect.
Is the telling of a raga of so little duration
that we do not always struggle with the scope of it?
Are the arguments of schools an idea that moves everybody?
An idea that no matter how dumb, still
comes from the First Dumbness?
Like far waters come from all parts. We love to salute
inept joy, however self-barking. Moreover, if stars
give a sense of the lore, if stars ache like stares,
only then will you prophesy the fiery end.

Move Through

for David

How dense the utter emptiness
of this body.
            What is the density of skin?
We can touch,
                    feel,
if we pay attention,
but our lives are stretched so thin
            here,
                    the particles so far apart.

How could such utter emptiness still produce a universe?
Now
        when everything's empty,
the universe expanding
from its original pinhead origins,
from this moment of loneliness
                        in the universe,
I am watching.

        In the emptiness
heavy oxygen in the blood
becomes huge and dangerous:
at each level
we must breathe out,
then breathe in,
when we dive down so far,
or come back.

In this universe
        something as big as a virus
can move through the most solid-seeming wall.
We cannot hear them, feel them,
tiny collisions of matter.

                    But all I want now
is the touch of your voice
in the vast dark,
        the sound of your skin.

Even in this familiar dimension,
just watching is acting.
Here the thin shadow of other dimensions
                    no longer matters,
        in this voice,
                    this urgency of self,
our own vast molecular spaces.

We Dance the Blue Right Out

We dance in shoes, in socks, in bare feet
We dance at weddings under Champagne corks
We dance below reunion moons
We dance in the dark

We dance the black footprints on the floor
We dance the box step our mothers taught us
We dance out the door and down the street

We dance Fred and Ginger
We dance Gene and the umbrella
We dance the face of Leslie Caron
We dance the rumba, the samba, the tarantella

We dance the clouds
We dance the rainbow in seven parts
We dance the snowflakes one at a time
We dance the stars

We dance touching bodies, hands
We dance without touching
We dance and you take off your coat
We dance and I take off my clothes

We dance sweating salt
We dance in skin
We dance all the flowers in the garden
We dance the peas, potatoes, broccoli, squash

We dance forever under the ground
We dance our coffins down
We dance the dirt clods' bounce, the rain
We dance the blue
right out of the
sky

What It Will Be Like

A mistranslation from César Vallejo

I will live in a city with walls made of light, of water,
where the tender fuchsias are never thirsty.

I will live in a city made of intricate wires and sand,
a city without flying paper or Kleenex,
a city of bread.
In my city the crusts will be chewy, sour—
golden stucco and brown shingle—
the heel of the loaf will be the curve of Land's End.

And in this glass of air
and clouds, my city will be dazzling, especially
when the light slips under the fog,
just before the glittering night.

The hills will be made with the bones of houses
and the gulls will fly up silently at night.
The only one awake will be my small black cat,
and his song will be so beautiful,
no one will ever be sad again.

What It Will Be Like

Before a Dinner Party

They come in, talking in low voices, the women
in their lace dresses, the men in dark blue
uniform coats crusted with gold.
The sharp bright smell of spices, scallions,
and their voices murmur over it, over
the candles, the chink of silver
on the white and gold Noritake plates,
while the white rice steams in mounds
at each end of the table.

In the shadows the damask tablecloth shines, napkins
press up to their red mouths, their smooth pink faces,
the condiments are passed with hums of appreciation.
Each small bowl recognized, saluted, dipped into
with silver spoons, tiny serving forks, until
dark yellow mustard pickle, chow chow,
chopped red tomatoes, fine green peppers
spill over their plates.

The centerpiece, the lazy Susan, my namesake, revolves
with its separate dishes; the bowls of dark shining pear
or mango chutney, slices of bananas,
orange sections, bits of peanut, egg,
sweet white coconut move around the room.

Chopping, chopping, days of chopping—all of us helping,
breathing in the rich yellow-brown smell from the small
red and white cans, curry, turmeric, mustard, cayenne
pepper—and beyond the gray Formica kitchen table
is the ochre color of the sky, of river slipping

past opened windows in Singapore, Baguio, Shanghai,
the Yellow River, and yellow curry shimmering in
the jade-green Süchow bowl, beside
the erect blue cat, the scarlet pigeon's-blood vase
brought back in crates before I was born,
in heavy trunks with strange labels, clasps, padlocks,
smells of excelsior, sandalwood, incense,
strange spices, packed by servants who moved
in far-off kitchens, slicing, chopping in some other
rhythm, some other lifetime without my existence.

They touched, my father, my mother, in dark corridors
of rocking steamships, across shifting oceans, walked
along silver decks under unfamiliar stars; they
slept in strange beds, sheets damp against their skin,
dreaming of other nights, of home, of flat, dusty fields,
and of neat gardens, geraniums, zinnias, marigolds.

They never dreamed of me, the middle daughter
listening to their voices murmuring in the other room
while I chopped scallions
in the kitchen
before a curry dinner.

Rainy Season Begins

This rain is new water
to us, new daughters to
these islands, new to such
rain.

The sky is full of water;
the whole yard ankle deep, water
falling down so fast, it has nowhere to go—
the ground under our bare feet is
water.

We lift our faces, our tongues catch it,
tiny cupfulls, warm water
on our hair, skin,
and we run, slide, splash waves
and oceans.

No more tight rubber boots,
no stiff, smelly raincoats,
no cold rain down the back,
dripping.

The sky is water and the air is water; we
breathe it, wear it, it splashes and swishes
and rushes and drums a beat for our dancing.
We dance in the water, new daughters to
this warm, silver rain.

March Planting

Time for potato tubers, leaf time,
root time, moon in first quarter, Taurus.
I plant corn and spinach, russets, carrots,
hoping the stars will pull the roots down
and the increasing moon will lift the leaves.
The work always takes longer than I think
and by the time I pull the furrow
across the bed, my fingers are trembling.
Many large seeds falter on the way
from my palm to their place.
Too many tiny black lettuces sprinkle out.
Sharp fat points, the three-dimensional spinach
seeds stick to the skin and fall right.
Smoothing over the bed with my hand,
my whole arm,
is the best part, and the watering
before night comes, the gentle crescent,
the sprinkle of stars.

Drive-Through

Even before I drive away,
I want one, I open
the red and yellow bag,
and there waiting, every identical
little squared and even
stick, nestled warm
and greasy, steamy—
I can feel the warmth
before we touch.

I pull one out,
lift it, and then
my mouth feels it,
that greasy heat,
slightly more
than the tongue can stand, so hot
the fingers can barely hold it.

So don't hold on,
quick, let it drop into your mouth.
Now it's that perfect hot grease and salt,
the outside salty, like the ocean,
like the perfect tear.
Then inside, on the tongue,
it's sweet, hot mush.

Take one or two, enough to fill the mouth,
one after the other, an endless

hot, salty stream.
I like to keep them
beside me on the seat, close,
just under my arm while I drive,
and when I'm done, I'm careful
with the evidence, scrunch up the bag,
brush off my fingers and my mouth,
so no one will suspect
my almost endless pleasure.

If chocolate

black shining,
        glazed thin, cracked like a frost
ice sheet
the square pan cools, the knife grates
into sugar crystallized, into warm
damp particles, black, deep,
                separate, the nuts are solid
and the middle is almost liquid,
blacker, ball
a crumb on your finger,

salty chocolate is sweeter,
and the mixing spoon is rough
to lick, salty,
ground coffee,
bitter, full brown-black
in the throat, and

chocolate floats low in the kitchen

Overcast Dilutes

Through the glass I am drinking at the window, today clearly shines from the third or fourth side and suddenly bounces in. Sometimes in rain, but not today, the books have rounded edges as though growing. The table leg, the chair, mass at the edge of the rug to hold the dark next, not sharply but evenly, as if pattern. Today does not show color. Dully under outside and here inside the overcast dilutes: I will pour and drink Berlioz in this light.

The Longing for Coffee

—the bitter
thick taste of it against the mouth
roof, the knowing
back of the tongue.

The black steam
rising silently, damp
cup warming the fingers, cheek,
bright, the bright—
        eyes opening after weeks of rain.

The lashes stick with waking salt.
Veins and passages,
blood and sound clear.
Light pulls me inside, and the taste
is the crumbling edge from the acrid binding
of a book left hidden on a high shelf.

And after such longing, there remains holding onto
the departing warmth, then only the cold and
remembered grounds.

Our Manatee Was a Younger Daughter

the plain one, left alone
among the tanks of bright-fringed polygala—
the proud anemone—phallic orange.
She was the silent one, even her waters
quiet around her. Turning slow
behind the glass, she was white-skinned
in the darkness, a moving cloud
like some whole imagined earth,
that blue marbled globe whose beauty
we never saw until we left her.

Turning soft, nuzzling,
paddling against the deeper dark,
she was alone in a corner tank
too small for any companion,
though even the blank-faced shark and rude-
lipped bass had company behind their glass.

When I first saw her,
she seemed to be looking back,
watching, floating in the midst of lettuce leaves.
But toward the end, after nights and years,
she turned away, sinking without motion,
and we hurried by, heading for the door,
all the echoing hordes of us.

Now when I pass that corner, that tank
is busy with small bright fish, rock caves,
and empty of her beauty.

I miss her heavy grace.

In the Academy of Sciences

> O no será la vida un pez / preparado para ser pájaro?
>
> —PABLO NERUDA

We walk past ancient towering ferns,
past jointed sticks of equisetum, dark redwood,
stiff ginkgo, ancient trees we hardly recognize,
but still here living to surprise us,
and past giant insects with half-bent legs
and bulging eyes we know too well.
We touch the gray stone casts of spiral snails
and brown rock bones of some huge fish
whose bulbous fins scraped the mud
to push out into breathing air.
We see the million-year-old narrow tracks
of worms, and next, the soaring reptile, fallen,
crumpled mud and bone, scales
or feathers, and what
we don't know is what's next.
Or will life not always be a fish
preparing to be a bird?

Tell Me

It's the first impulse. When you're a child, you come in the door and say, "I want to tell you something." If you're lucky, somebody says, "What?"

—GRACE PALEY

Is Anger a Question?

Smash the glass free from
    closed vision, free to see, free
        to sweep up glass

Smash the brake pedal to the floor
    jam the wheel, curb the children, free
        the silence, free the long drive home

Bang the pots and pans on the shelf
    bend the pot lid, wake
        the husband, free
            from silence
                free from single sleep

Free the pots, the pans
bang the anger
rattle the husband
pot the silence
sleep the single shelf

since you ask, I don't remember

SINCE:	because on account of
YOU:	(are) too bossy too prying too invading wouldn't understand wouldn't try to understand wouldn't want to couldn't already know this
ASK:	beg plead query test
I:	ego shell self the one who the other
DON'T:	contraction (conversational) do not can't don't want to wouldn't even if I could (and keep my self intact) so I won't

REMEMBER: call it up
people that time with memories
thoughts
create bits that make historical sense
make up facts
lie

Women Talk

We talk,
every day talk,
a never-ending stream of words,
no sudden breaks,
no piles of stones,
no logs across the stream;
no, we make channels for each other's words:
here, bring it this way,
no, watch out for that one,
that way lies danger, where
the words hurt or stop;
here, this is the way,
this old familiar path;
your day, like yesterday,
oh not of the children that never call,
or the one who moved in with his girl;
tell me what you're doing tomorrow,
or what you cooked, what you wore,
who came, who called, what you
talked about, what you thought or hoped
or dreamed, tell me about your dream,
and I'll give you my recipe for lemon chard
and the letter I got, the call I made;
slowly, carefully around the edges,
we keep to the middle; with time
it will deepen and fill with
tears, with flowers.

San Diego, April 25, 1942

The day before I was born was a day of hats,
and waiting for the word and packing bags.
My father was out at sea; my sisters went to aunts,
Evie, Dot, and Vivian; it was a women's world of black-
outs and rationed gas, so they arranged an April
birth, induced by Navy doctors, two weeks early.

The day before I was born, my sisters were up early
and dressed in clean white socks, Sunday coats and hats.
It was cold that California April;
they put woolen booties, pink baby blankets, in the bag
and closed it, lugged it down to the old black
Ford. They drove past poppy-orange hills to hours of aunts,

my grandmother's sisters, Neet, Judd, Berenice. The aunts
were waiting for them, smoking and talking, talking. Early
news from the Russian front was black,
and they passed around a picture: in strange fur hats,
my grandfather and someone carrying his envoy's bags
with the official baggage stamps in the cold Russian April.

That night no one talked about my father's ship held in April
storms, but my slow and heavy mother worried. The aunts
talked carefully, smoked and drank, carried her bag.
It wasn't spring for him on his ship with his early

orders to the Aleutians; in pictures he wore the khaki hat
of working ships, not the brass and black.

The day before I was born they ate black-
skinned avocados fallen in the yard that April,
ripened inside golden green, with skin like hats,
like German helmets, flesh scooped out by aunts
and fed to children whom they sent to bed early,
while they smoked, talked into the night. At dawn her bag

was carried down, put in a taxi to go to the Base, her bag
with pale nightgown, robe, Nero Wolfe. That old black
bag was beside the bed when the first visitors came early
and stayed to talk and smoke in the hospital room that April
night and to tap at me on the nursery glass. All the aunts
took turns peeking around the nurses' stiff white hats.

Into what a world of war, and bags, and April
I was born, the old black Ford, my sisters, all those aunts,
early, in a woman's world of stylish, tilted, brave, and funny hats.

Laundry

I never touched their bodies, only their clothes. Every week I hung them out, watched stains appear, disappear. My sisters' crinolines dripped blue globs of starch. Lace nightgown, my father's immense striped shorts, my mother's lilac-flowered dress, yellowing bra. Granddaddy the admiral unpacked his regulation BVDs and brought them down for the wash. I admired them, the thin knitted skin, the shape of his shoulder blades, hips. Such power, humming over the immanence of underwear. He sang to me, "And his name was Napoleon, all on account of his bony parts."

Everywhere, I've put up lines: across camp, around the red cedar, above the raw garden on Hope Street, at the back of the apartment parking-lot slope over the cinders and trash cans. When I hang up laundry, the proof is in the line of clean work done. I made up my first lines playing in the laundry basket, singing in with the clean clothes. Soap flakes, white cotton, sunlight, smell of clean, not bleach, not new. Satisfaction snaps with the corner of the drying sheet. On good summer days you can hang two loads, one after you take down the other. In winter the gauze diapers freeze crisp before you reach the end of the row.

Laundry is the wet gesture against the evil eye of backyards: *shirt, pants, blouse, dish towel, sock, sock, pillowcase, sheet.* The incantation of cloth lies across the empty sky, yards. Everywhere the lines stretch out with the weight.

Weaving: Outdoor Installation Along the Road

> *The current Landmarks Exhibition . . . presents three site-specific works in . . . the Marin Headlands. . . . The fiber artist Gyöngy Laky has super-imposed upon the landscape three separate grid pieces made of colorful plastic surveyor's tape . . . limited to the primary colors because she wanted them to stand out boldly against the mixed colors of nature.*
>
> —CHARLES MIEDZINSKI, *Artweek*

1.

The weaver begins the piece by exact measurement.
She bends over the nails, anchoring, tapping into the ground.
She ties the blue surveyor's tape to the nail,
lays out the first line across the grass strip
at the crossroads, the one all the others will match,
not stretching so that the line will not bend.

Other weavers move back and forth, calling
to each other, straighten it out, straight, higher, closer,
then the cross rows under and over,
the rolls of tape pass across the nearly level ground,
the rounding curves of the intersection.

For now the blue weaving holds the ground,
the water of Rodeo Lagoon, the morning sky.

2.

They weave red tape into a figure eight
beside the road, inside and outside the double circle
horses have worn in the short grass,
a riding ring. Weaving fills the ground,
begins and ends at the path,

the red crossings become ground,
the worn dirt rounds the figure.

3.
Yellow on the steep hill, wildflowers, drying grass,
the sudden bloom of moss, sunlight. Closer,
it is the woven patch, a mending on the hill.

To rest, the weavers crawl under it,
lie on their backs against the steep slope.
Looking up through the giant yellow grid,
they feel the weight of the work against the body.
Every strand is felt by its connection to every other strand.
The weight is comforting, as hand weaving is
warm, even unevenness.

4.
When we drive along the road, at the curve
we are struck by the bright blue, so human made,
by the red warming us until we leave it in the mirror,
and the yellow just out of the corner of the eye.

The disturbed public eye, expecting the precise
military roads, signs, buildings, or only
the natural hills, will protest, blink again. After
official delays and official permits and officials,
the weavers have tapped each nail in with such care
into the rough ground, woven every line, every piece

without a loosening, so that to remove it would also
take such care.

5.
To rip each piece
out, the vandal
had to weave back and
forth, pull
it out in lines;
the woven order
imposed on him
one moment of destructive
joy.

Down the road the horses were restless,
the animals disturbed, he
was heard.

6.
Tomorrow in the light, the constant
sea wind will blow across the long salt hay.
The sea grass will bend itself
into the under/over pattern.

The steep hillsides, the cloud
shadows make the yellow,
the red, the blue; and the remembered
weavings are still there, the surprise

of rounding the corner, coming
up on color, pattern, sudden
in the wild headlands.

The Muskrats at Giverny

When Monet died in Giverny in the fall of 1926,
the garden and the pool slowly died with him.
—STEPHEN SHORE, *The Gardens at Giverny*

The muskrats watch an oily residue
collect in the depressions
along the crumbling edge of the pond.
The bridge is silent;
no more slow and halting
footsteps echoing. Wisteria twists
into heavy knots too thick
to bloom. Every day
the bench is empty, even
at sunset when he used to sit and watch,
his heavy feet spread wide apart and
always on the same worn spot.
Now the lilies are eaten down to the bulbs,
and the narcissus; the rose thorns
harden and die. The path is filled with
nasturtium; black leaves and empty seed pods
rattle in the wind. Under the trees
the smell of dusk.

Fallen branches, dark leaves
block the crumbling sluice gate,
and the waters of the little Epte
no longer spill over into the still pond
to rock the water lilies. Every day
the pond seems smaller than before:
the muskrats will soon leave

their stick-filled nests to search
farther down the damp and rotting empty paths.

And when the long dark spring comes again,
the muskrats at Giverny will give birth
to their young and groom their rough
and scented fur. And they will sing to the kits
of the remembered blues and greens
of their youth, of iris stem and lily bud.
But the only promise is
the fine-haired pale green silk of nettle.

She Waited as If It Might Come to Him: Rye, October 1907

Theodora Bosanquet arrived punctually at ten, after a steep walk up through the narrow crossing streets of Rye. Her neat linen skirt was tucked under the desk, and her competent brown boots kept time with the long sentences, the tapping keys. At last Henry James faced the constant listener with, in every way, perfect discretion.

"Let us begin with John Marcher, begin with 'The Beast in the Jungle':

"*She waited as if it might come to him, but as, only meeting her eyes in wonder, he gave no sign, she burnt her ships.*

'Has it ever happened?' "

His hair still damp and glistening from his bath, he rolled forth words, foaming blue translucent breakers toppling. Eyes on the commas, the dashes, the vast alert universe, he rounded the corner of the blotter.

"It was impossible he shouldn't take to himself that she was really interested, though it all kept coming as perfect surprise. He had thought of himself so long as abominably alone and lo he wasn't alone a bit...."

She got every word. The admirable machine tapped the lines smoothly. Pages pressed between the rollers, lifted into the room.

In each lengthening pause between dictations, the pages of her book rustled over softly, rhythmically marking off the time in the silent, still, blest world. Her blue bicycle waited at the door under the old white rose. The clock stood between the tall windows, the clear light.

Two Alices

A mistranslation

I thought there were two Alices. In 1913, an Alice stroked her brother's hair and thought sometimes he lived like a Mona Lisa. On the top floor it seemed like a painting, all street and balcony and music. But once in a while the calendar seemed drawn down around her face like curtains. And so the maid, also named Alice, had glimpsed a couple of drops, little ones, on the vanity. For herself, it seemed she could hear them talking about her own, about her hairpins, about the little pines, about everything still down there on the street.

It Is the Edge of All

IN MEMORY / SYLVIA PLATH HUGHES / 1932–1963 /
EVEN AMIDST FIERCE FLAMES / THE GOLDEN LOTUS
CAN BE PLANTED

—Gravestone inscription, Heptonstall churchyard, Yorkshire

Even now, every young girl has this:
the edges, the quick core
that sings
but only for this moment.
And whether
it is the edge of all
that has gone before
or the thin hard rind
of what is to be
will only be revealed after,
when it no longer matters.

It was only when the poet
began without the list
of subjects written out for her,
began without the thesaurus
in her lap, the unabridged dictionary.
Only then did she voice
that bright and funny, bitter
note, deep in the throat,
that was her own.

A wind blows through her
now, her long legs
are dust, her dark hair
is no longer brushed back

from her face but lies wound
about her bones,
cradling that hollowing skull
in the dark simplicity,
the death that was always waiting
under the common family headstone,
carved with words that lie.
We are not deceived by them,
or the pages and pages of words:
mother's, husband's, lover's,
professor's, doctor's.
The silence of the lost journal lies
empty in our mouths. But
she

has written for us, and
no young girl need ever have this
cruel promise, these cruel lies again.
She has written,
and we have only to listen
to come to the edge of ourselves, so
ungathered, so full of desire.

Shame, My Dark Sister,

to you, Tlatzolteotl,
I bring my lies and every act
of hate and cowardice, of deceit and pride,
the hiding and the taking,
    the holding on, the letting go.
Now I bring to you the hours of blank
confusion, of not feeling
the loss, and the forgetting,
all the nights of my shame,
that deep vibration.

I bring it all to you, Filth Eater,
Merciful Devourer.
I hold back nothing
    from you.
You were with me at every crossroad,
waiting with the Four Sisters who urged me
to take the wrong road, lost
in desire in all my times,
the girl-child who wrestled boys,
the virgin who dreamed and danced in moonlight,
the mother who gave away her second child and kept silent,
the grandmother who holds still,
    still trying to remember and forgive.

I look on your horrible beauty, your black mouth,
your ancient vulture head, red throat, the dark night wings,

the bleeding from your belly,
your vulva, your wing claws, your talons:
no defilement too great to be forgiven.

Dark Sister, tear me open, untwist
me and set my heart straight,
fold me into your loving arms.

Child of Ice

My War

There was no safe place; it was wartime San Francisco.
My mother and my sisters and I waited
in the flat on Union Street, a flat full of windows,
of anger, worry, and broken china,
waited for my father to come back with his ship.
For us there was nowhere else:
everyone had to wait and do what we were told.
During the blackouts, over and over I asked:
why did we cover the windows with heavy wool blankets?
Why couldn't we leave a light on in the dark?

To come inside, we pushed open the heavy glass front door
that would give us no protection if they came up our street.
Ours was the upper flat, up two flights and down the hall,
the living room with its white walls and bookshelves,
its sofa and tables and chairs, the sofa I am sitting on now.
Watching for my sisters to come home from school,
I looked out the window, at the bay
with its lines of gray ships passing silently
under the bridge, none of them my father's.

At night I walked down the hall the other way, to the darker
back of the flat, past my sisters' room,
past my mother's room with her high bed,
a lighted cigarette in the ashtray on her mirrored dresser.
I went to the next room, my room, and my big bed
with its pink taffeta quilt, puffed up, slippery. It made noise,
it slid off sideways, it smelled like dog pee and like
the long night breathing in the dark.

Speaking of Jochabed

I know
she must have come back, later, just at dusk when
the shadows in the rushes were taller than a man,
and she must have heard a rustling, voices
whispering she couldn't quite understand.

She must have searched thoroughly, remembering
the exact spot. But of course the river had kept on rising—
it was spring, what did she expect? And the dark leaves
must have slashed her arms
where she pushed through.

The basket/he was gone, as she expected,
pushing back the leaves to see the empty place.
Had he been taken to a better home?
to a father and a mother who could give him
soft clothes, pomegranates, oranges and honey,
raise him up to be their son, no longer hers,
not even of her?

She must have washed the mud from her hands and feet
in the dark, rushing water and climbed the bank
to walk the river road back into a reddened sky.

Scopolamine

after a poem by Catherine Pozzi

The drug sliding into my vein
has flooded my heart and sweeps it away;
out in the open I shall have to steer carefully,
floating there inside an unmanageable heart,
out where forgetting spreads like honey.

I ignore the cold room and the rough white sheets,
someone shaving between my legs, my screaming.
My mind's voice floats away, my body left behind,
the part that "remembers" drifts in "twilight sleep,"
in distilled nightshade, purple star-flower, lost time.

The body is still anchored back there, the cells remembering.
Tissues act, the heart pumps, ears take in
the metallic clang of sterile pans
to be used for what is expelled: urine,
blood, feces, placenta, roots of children.

Child of Ice

EARLY JUNE

Linoleum floor, each gray
square barred by a thin slant
of street light through the blinds.
He and I sit in darkness
in opposite chairs
placed along the walls
of the waiting room. There are
posters of teeth.

END OF JANUARY

Spring is born in the blood,
moving slow with tearing thought.

The roots are gray and still with ice.
I will bear to give up this child.

Darkness in the blood-black womb.
Passing, passed. A minute

in light I hold her and
I will bear to give up this child.

Spring is gone from my blood.
The roots are still, the bud brown-tipped.

If only I could
I would

see her stand small and singing,
dark in light, light in dark.

FEBRUARY NIGHT

The child of ice dreams
still in my arms, sleeping warm.
Ice slides in waves across
the midnight river, ridged deep,
dark water moving slow as memory.
    I call across the river, though
    I cannot save us both.

Every night breaks in glacier waves
over and over the frozen river,
and I save her, lift
her up to other arms,
a gift I cannot change.
    I call across the river, though
    I cannot save us both.

My frozen arms crack where they bend.
I will slip beneath the river,
the black water thick with silence.
I cannot hear the other still and distant voices.
I will remember this cold night.
    I call across the river.
    I cannot save us both.

In Dreams

Where do the things in dreams go?
In my dreams things seem
to remain still, immovable,
waiting for me to come.

What, then, does move in your dreams?
My hand moves, my feet,
sometimes my whole body.
I can turn my head to look.

What is there to look at?
The furniture, the staircases, the doorways,
some things
I must choose among.

How do you know which one to choose?
The doorknob comes to my hand.
The stairs lead to somewhere I want to go,
folding back and back on themselves.

Are these all familiar places you have known?
Often, like the too-steep attic stairs
they used to warn me about, or the sharp-edged
granite steps of the college library.

Did they often warn you of dangers that you still had to face?
The steepness was in my eyes,
I think they were ordinary,
just the stairs to everyone else.

Is there anyone else there in your dreams?
My son when he was little, 2½ or three.
He would come with me up all those stairs,
I'd hold his hand and we would count.

Do you hear people talk, hear their words?
No, he was so good, he hardly made a sound,
especially in the Reading Room with me,
because there was no other place for him to go.

Do you remember the silence?
I liked his quiet then, though now I want him to talk.
I want him to tell me everything.
I want him to tell me his dreams.

In February Rain: A Boy

a sudden shout
something heavy
crashes against the wall

a door slams
and it's cold in the rest of the house

his music
    a beat
pulses faint through wood

now his door opens again
the rush of sound is the rain of rain
loud, rain
overflowing,
filling all the space,
the gutters roar, the street
is a hill
of water rushing

now he wants to eat
everything, anything,
his hunger
the devouring cold after us
we feed him everything, even the wind

and everything
at last
becomes still
    his sudden hug
the green green hills

Three Sketches

1. Forgiveness

white
not without color
not clear
    or translucent
but white
that smooth blank
    nothing there
    no credit
no blame

2. Longing

not loss
not emptiness
but wanting
    thin
    narrow faces, bodies
    charcoal on white

3. Tenderness

the garden, early evening
the children coming inside
the mother holding the baby,
his pale foot,
unmarked skin held carefully,
the mother sitting on the step
the child curving into her shoulder,
her arm curving him into her

In That Dark Wood

In the night wood, I walked blindly, feeling my way
through the empty air, listening for faint voices
drifting up without direction from the path.

If I missed the turn, I could walk for miles, lost;
the forest went on and on. I could not see, and so I slowed
to stare into the dark, and staring, found it darker.

I stopped, afraid to go on, afraid to go back,
when suddenly
    silent wings brushed past.

It was a lifting of the dark: my fear drew back
and I could see. It was a coming of the light,
coming to me in that dark wood.

At the End, When You Speak

do not praise me for exceptional
kindness, for I thought
to give more than I received,
not seeing that I have been
given everything, everything.

Do not wonder either at my good fortune or
my suffering; only now do I
begin to see how each contains the other, how
the birth of each of my daughters is
inseparable,
somehow,
from the other's loss.

And fame, that red berry
just beyond reach among the thorns—
say I watched it wither, blacken, pecked by
birds and left to rot,
still out of reach,
still not understood.

Say instead
I learned to live with hidden
chocolate, bread baking
in the oven, children
singing in the back seat
all the way home.

Notes

"In the Academy of Sciences": The epigraph, and the last two lines of the poem translating it, are taken from *"No será nuestra vida un túnel,"* in *The Book of Questions* by Pablo Neruda, translated by William O'Daly, reprinted here with the permission of Copper Canyon Press, and of the Neruda estate.

Theodora Bosanquet, referred to in "She Waited as If It Might Come to Him," was Henry James's third amanuensis, or literary secretary, and stayed with him for nine years typing his works from dictation until his death in the spring of 1916. The title, quotations and italicized paragraphs contained within the text, as well as some of the factual details, are taken from the diaries and other writings of Theodora Bosanquet, and from letters and a short story by Henry James, "The Beast in the Jungle."

"It Is the Edge of All" was written as a response while working on three-part collaborative pieces with Terry Ehret and Steve Gilmartin, and some lines have been shared between those poems.

"Shame, My Dark Sister": Tlatzolteotl is the Aztec goddess of reincarnation, of blood and darkness, of mothering, aging, of death and rebirth. "Anything that can overwhelm and destroy us also has the power to heal and grant forgiveness." (John Mini, *The Aztec Virgin: The Secret Mystical Tradition of Our Lady of Guadalupe,* Trans-Hyperborean Institute of Science Publishing, 2000.)

"Speaking of Jochabed": Jochabed was the mother of Moses, who gave up her son so that he could be found by Pharaoh's daughter and all the prophecies could be fulfilled, as in the stories of the sacred king, the fatherless hero, who first had to be born of the waters and set afloat on the river in a basket of rushes to begin the many miracles of his life.

"Scopolamine" was written in response to the first stanza of a poem of the same name by Catherine Pozzi, friend of Rilke and Gide, lover of Paul Valéry.

About the Author

Susan Herron Sibbet lives with her husband in San Francisco in a flat next to Argonne Community Garden, with berry bushes and fruit trees they planted more than twenty years ago. She was a Woodrow Wilson Fellow and a Bunting Fellow at Radcliffe/Harvard, and has held writing residencies at Soapstone in Oregon and the Headlands Center for the Arts in California. She has taught in the California Poets in the Schools program in Bay Area schools for many years.

Sixteen Rivers Press is a shared-work, not-for-profit poetry collective dedicated to providing an alternative publishing avenue for San Francisco Bay Area poets. Founded in 1999 by seven women writers, the press is named for the sixteen rivers that flow into San Francisco Bay.

San Joaquin ~ Fresno ~ Chowchilla ~ Merced ~ Tuolumne
Stanislaus ~ Calaveras ~ Bear ~ Mokelumne ~
Cosumnes ~ American ~ Yuba ~ Feather ~ Sacramento
Napa ~ Petaluma